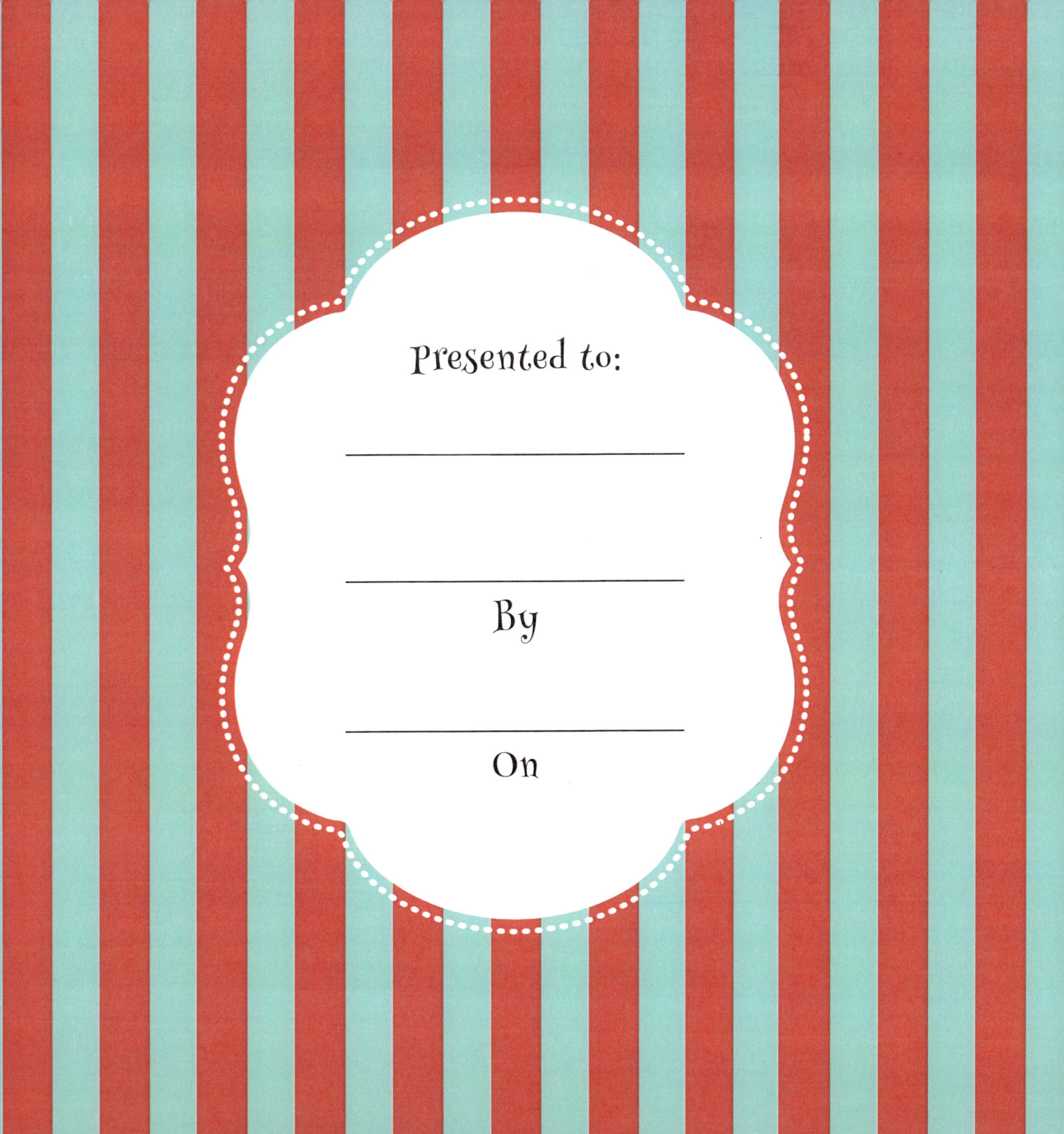

Dedication

To my grandchildren; Dylan and Avery; and to my nephew and niece; Matty and Lilly. You are the youngest generation of our family. I pray this work will inspire you as you have inspired me.

Published by WiseOwl, An Imprint of Tole Publishing LLC
Copyright © 2020 by Chris Kramer

All rights reserved. No part of this book may be reproduced, stored in a retrieval system, or transmitted in any form or by any means-electronic, mechanical, photocopying, recording, or otherwise, without written permission from the publisher.

ISBNS: 978-1-948696-14-2 (Paperback), 978-1-9486896-15-9 (Hardback), 978-1-9486896-17-3 (Kindle)
Library of Congress Control Number: 2020943586

Scripture quotations are from the ESV® Bible (The Holy Bible, English Standard Version®), copyright © 2001 by Crossway, a publishing ministry of Good News Publishers. Used by permission. All rights reserved.

Cover and Interior Images: AdobeStock: Zoo animals © GraphicsRF, Frog with tongue sticking out © brgfx, Polar Bear © tigatelu, Singing Turtle © Visual Generation, Dog with blue collar © Anna Velichkovsky, Oranges © Emil, Dog smelling flower © Yael Weiss, Monkey © irwanjos, Elephants © Амитрий Ковыршов, Dinosaur with kite © Morphart, Kangaroo © tigatelu, Happy House © grafico2011, Goldfish © Christos Georghiou, Smiling Frog © jihane37, Bunny © tigatelu, Cat in car © Muza_art, Caterpillar © Christos Georghiou, Treasure map © GraphicsRF, Igloo © Anna Velichkovsky , Pig © tigatelu, Dog taking bath © tigatelu, Queen Bee © Ruangdesign19, Cat with umbrella © ruksina, Running turtle © GuGGGar, Penguin © tigatelu, Owl and chalkboard © orensila, Paper texture © flas100, Children learning © tigatelu

Printed in the United States of America

TOLE PUBLISHING, PO BOX 1098,
MORGANTOWN, KY. 42261-8411
www.tolepublishing.com

I Can Rhyme!

Fill-in-the-Blank Poems

With Answer Key in the Back of the Book

Chris Kramer

Bb Cc Dd Ee
Gg Hh Ii Jj
Ll Mm Nn Oo
Pp Qq Rr Ss
Tt Uu Vv Ww
Xx Yy Zz

Aa

Math is how we learn to count.
Learning makes us glad.
Subtraction is to take away.
Addition is to A___.

Bb

Little things that fly and crawl;
Some hide under rugs.
They're in the sky, in trees, up walls;
They're insects we call B_____.

Cc

We drive along from place to place,
Sometimes it's near or far.
To see our loved ones face to face
We go there in a C____.

Dd

Our pets are animals that we love
And take for walks and jogs.
They "meow" and they "ruff-ruff."
They are our cats and D____.

Ee

Our eyes can see a day so clear.
Our mouths make sounds so others hear.
Our hands can reach for what is near.
To listen we must use our E____.

Ff

He leaps along across the way.
He hops upon a log.
Lily pads are where he plays.
"Ribbit," goes a F____.

Gg

We have feelings as a child;
When we cry we're sad.
Happy feelings make us smile;
And smiling shows we're G_____.

Hh

A house is where we live and play,
Too far we will not roam.
We share our lives with family.
We call our house a H_____.

Winter brings the cold and snows;
A warm coat is so nice.
We bundle up our hands and toes
So we won't freeze like I____.

Exercise is what you need.
Don't sit there like a lump!
Walk and run and play and swing,
Bounce and leap and J_____.

Kk

Made with paper, sticks, and string,
It's ready to take flight.
Colors, paints, and pretty things,
Look up! There flies a K____.

Ll

We should be nice to everyone.
We never push or shove.
We must be kind and good and fun
With feelings we call L____.

Mm

They eat bananas and they swing
On branches high up in the trees.
They play and smile at what they see;
Our silly friends are called M_____.

Nn

I breathe air in and breathe air out
And smell flowers like a rose.
If it gets stuffy there's no doubt
I must blow my N____.

Healthy foods are good for you;
Like veggies, soup, or porridge.
Some are sweet and yummy too;
Like an apple or an O_____.

Pp

They oink and squeal and roll about.
In the mud they dig.
They're plump and round and have a snout.
We call them hogs or P____.

Qq

A woman sits upon a throne;
She's kind and never mean.
She wears a crown upon her head;
Her people call her Q_____.

Rr

We need to play out in the sun.
Here are some things to do for fun:
Jump and play, say "three, two, one,"
Then hop and skip and leap and R____.

Ss

When you think a happy thought,
Show it with some style.
Show you're happy with your mouth;
With it, you can S_____.

Tt

In your mouth it sits among
Rows of teeth since you were young.
You need it when a song is sung.
You also taste things with your T_____.

Uu

Sometimes the skies are dark around
With lightning, wind, and thunder.
Umbrellas when the rain comes down
Protect you when you're U_____.

When others hear me talk or sing
I must make a choice.
To speak real loud or quietly,
Do I lower or raise my V____?

Ww

We wash ourselves, our clothes, and pets.
We splash and play, but don't forget
To grab a towel 'cause you can bet
That water makes you very W_____.

Xx

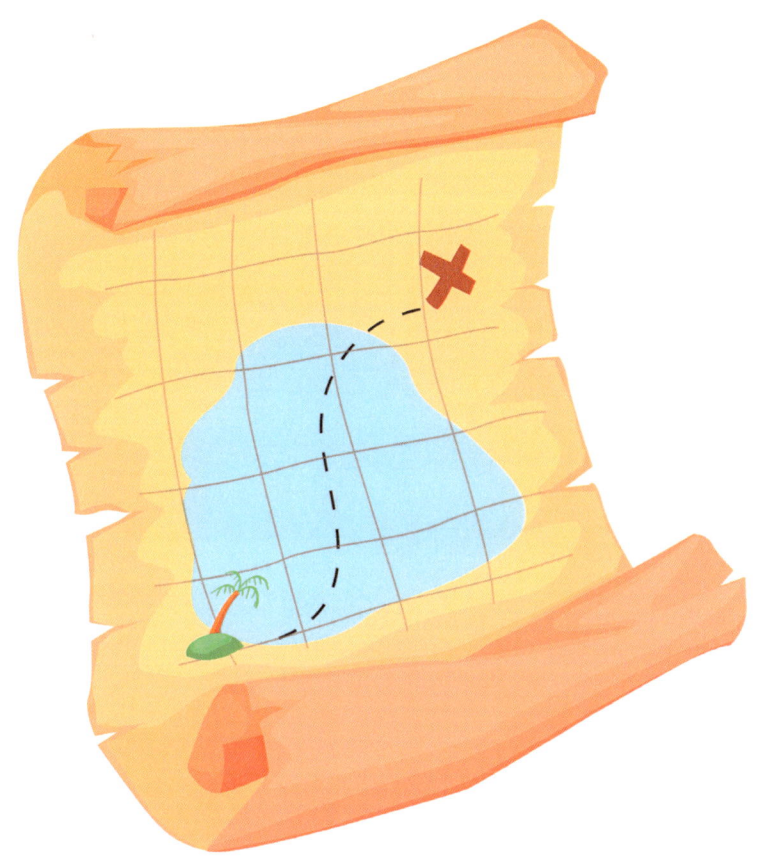

A treasure hunt is fun to play,
It makes us all perplexed.
To find it on a treasure map
The spot is marked with ___.

It could mean I'm really hungry,
When I get gurgles in my tummy.
A snack, some food, please give me something
That tastes so good and very Y_____.

Zz

There is a place that we can go
And learn something that's new.
About fish and birds and animals
Who live down at the Z___.

Answer Key

A: Add
B: Bugs
C: Car
D: Dogs
E: Ears
F: Frog
G: Glad
H: Home
I: Ice
J: Jump
K: Kite
L: Love
M: Monkeys

N: Nose
O: Orange
P: Pigs
Q: Queen
R: Run
S: Smile
T: Tongue
U: Under
V: Voice
W: Wet
X: X
Y: Yummy
Z: Zoo

Chris Kramer lives in Clarksville, Tennessee, and has been a gospel preacher for thirty years. He and his wife have three children, and they are blessed with two bright grandchildren. Inspired by his grandchildren, Chris hopes to share that inspiration to a new generation to be happy, well rounded, and creative. In his writings, he desires all to see God's beauty in this world through the eyes of a child. And in doing so, help inspire all to have childlike faith.

Would you like to reach out to Chris? You can contact him at *chriskramer@tolepublishing.com*. He would love to hear from you!

Jesus said, "Let the little children come to me and do not hinder them, for to such belongs the kingdom of heaven." Matthew 19:14, ESV

www.ingramcontent.com/pod-product-compliance
Lightning Source LLC
Chambersburg PA
CBRC091503220426
43661CB00021B/1305